DACITE, DARKNESS, AND DIVINITIES DIALOGUE

(Poetry in the mourn /morn)

WRITTEN BY
ANGELA PSALM

©2024 Dacite, Darkness, and Divinities Dialogue
(Poetry in the mourn / morn)

Author: Angela Psalm

Co-editors:
Kindra M Austin, Kristy Johnson & Brandy Lane
All rights reserved.

Foreword by: Stuti Sinha

Printed in Australia.

This is a work of fiction. Names, places, characters or incidences are the product of the author's imagination or are used fictitiously. Any resemblance to actual persons, living or dead, events, or locale is entirely coincidental. No part of this book may be used, stored in a system retrieval system, or transmitted, in any form or any means—by electronic, mechanical, photocopying, recording, or reproduced in any manner whatsoever—without written permission from the author, except in the case of brief quotations embodied in critical articles and reviews.

ISBN: 978-969-43-9245-5
Library of Congress Control Number: 2024913268

Published in Australia by:
The Dungeon Keep Atheneum Pty Ltd
Book design:
Evagelia Newell

Illustrations: SueAnn Summers @the_musing_palette
Front Cover Center: •Radiant Rhizomes
Interior Illustrations: •Nyx's Mirror •Icarus
•Ecliptic Conversation •Dryad •Mistress

Publishing Consultant:
Formatting, additional edits,
cover color matching, and layout design.
Brandy Lane of Where Beautiful Inks LLC.

All other decorative art throughout this book is licensed through Canva and Canva Pro memberships.

DEDICATION

I would like to dedicate my first solo publication to my husband Chris and twin soul son Erek who have endured the countless hours of being my sounding board and who understand my love of word. We are a communal collection of creativity.

To all the incredible writers who I have read over the years and to all of those whom I have met during the years of lockdown, you have inspired, saved, and allowed me to be the person I have always been.

To those who dream, it is never too late to realise them.

AUTHOR'S NOTE

I would like to acknowledge the inspirational poets, communities, and pages on Instagram with their prompts and active lives. I thank you. You inspired a lot of these pieces as well as helping me find my way home.

Angela Psalm

EPIGRAPH

IN THE BEGINNING OF FREE

In the beginning of Free – dom,
she sought solace in her empty shell,
her heart—a capsule of butterflies.
While enjoying life, she caught Eros's desires.
Eros was a vacuous heartbreak lothario,
caught on a whimper and transfixed on Free – dom.
He burned for her, he needed her
while he drank the sanguine of a lover's wine.
Alas Free - dom knew too well of Eros,
she would rather be empty and whole,
than full of broken promises and pain.
High above in the heavenly, sky she was safe.

Eros obsessed with the capture of Free – dom.
He asked Mythos to help in the treachery.
He was happy to corrupt the sanctity of love.
Eros was a fool to believe that Free - dom would subjugate.
The fine line between love and hate
was drawn between the brothers Eros and Mythos,
but Free - dom learnt to never cross that line—
Instead, floats above in the peace of the heavenly sky.

ILLUSTRATIONS BY
Sue Ann Summers

Mistress
Logo

Radiant Rhizomes
Cover Art and Title Page.

Dryad
Pg. 1 Full-color
Pgs. 2-4 Mirrored and with transparency.

Ecliptic Conversation
Pg. 5 Full-color
Pgs. 6-26 Half pictures with transparency.

Nyx's Mirror
Pg. 27 Full-color
Pgs. 28-68 Mirrored and with transparency.

Icarus
Pg. 69
Pgs. 70-102 Mirrored and with transparency.

A NOTE FROM
Sue Ann Summers

RADIANT RHIZOMES

Rhizomes are another word for, "roots." Angela's writing draws from her heritage, is magnificently cerebral, syllogizes light and shadow, and radiates with glorious empowerment. Her birthstone shines against the roots, and snowdrops begin to thrive under her care, representing her generous reach and the beautiful energy she shares with us all. This image portrays more than just a celestial giant, it is an honorable nod to the vastness of Angela's spirit.

FOREWORD

I am sure we have all cursed, or found safety in or flirted with both in the pandemic and subsequent lockdown.

For me, it was more finding safety, finding myself and discovering new connections, in the un-physical online world. Of the many connections I made, there are a handful now that have become intimate and powerful friendships. Angela is undoubtedly in that special handful. It is through the beginnings of that friendship that I also discovered her love affair with delicious darkness, and expressing that in written word.

Although I have never heard Angela say this, she is who I would describe as a natural and vivid storyteller. One of the pieces I read in the early period of getting to know her was a piece titled Little Boy Blue - a gut-wrenching confession of her emotions in the process of child loss as a young mother and the subsequent grief.

"....*the echoing of sobs, painful sobs, sorrowful sobs. I hear them every night from a young girl giving birth to an angel that grew their wings before their first breath, an angel I still talk to, especially on my hard days, the one no one knew had existed. All anyone knew was the extra weight I put on and when I lost you, my physical walls disappeared and I was lost, so I ate finding comfort in the new walls I built, unhealthy pretending you were still in my womb.*"

continued

I very quickly realized that there are many layers to Angie's writing and, as a reader, if you really want to dive into the emotional variety of her words, that's impossible to get by reading one or two pieces. If you're discovering her for the first time through this book, you are likely to go on a binge read in the beginning in a curious exploration of her versatility, as I once did. Getting to know Ang; her softness, her toughness and the wide spectrum in between is being able to see her in the words she writes; a unique gift I treasure of knowing her both as a writer but also as someone very dear to my heart.

'Siren', one of the early pieces in this book, is, in my mind, a classic representation of Angela as a person, a dreamer and a writer. The opening lines of the piece throw the reader, unhesitatingly, into roiling agony and devastation.

"That day I threw away the key. in a drunken haze of rage. Destroyed by you-I lay on the floor.
I ask myself, How did our love turn to hate?"

You are then taken on a journey that is replete with unmissable flairs of poetic brilliance in lines like "*A month lost without the algorithm to speak*" and "*My looking glass was shattered from the lucid ambiance of heart's end.*"

And before long, this piece becomes a smoothly told narrative of courage and resurrection in the face of despair and defeat.

"I will not allow love to be a weakness.
...I will never fear that which is endless.
Let the darkness you cast upon me, burn... burn... and cleanse away the impure.
For I will continue to believe, in the magic of happiness..."

While this will feel like a familiar plotline, it is the charisma of Angela's narrative and her ability to pull the reader into her world— that will envelop you as the reader.

A piece like Labyrinth is raw and confessional as seen in lines like

"The search is in the hope of you:
to find the pieces of your soul set adrift in time—
fractured due to my selfish and displeasing actions."

Yet, at the same time, it manages to dance delicately on the edge of pain and hope.

"...the bones of hope hold on even though there are scars stitched across my soul."

It mirrors the condition of experiencing events in our life through layers of emotions that are apparently even in conflict, rather than a singular emotion. In her work often, as in this piece, hope eventually triumphs.

"So yes, I bear the scars across my timeless soul,
but it is you, Hope, that I am blessed to know. My guiding light."

Ang doesn't dabble in poetry. She immerses herself in it every day. I have often heard her say - "I just need to get this off my chest and write it out", just one of the things amongst many that reminds me that this isn't someone who discovered writing, but actually, she is a writer, who uses her medium to discover herself, ground herself and make sense of her world.

I hope that as you turn the pages of Angie's debut poetry collection, 'Dacite, Darkness and Divinities Dialogue' you will feel like you are getting to know Angela and yourself a little more.

Stuti Sinha
IG: @stutisinha__
(Published and award winning writer of fiction and poetry)

TABLE OF CONTENTS

I, DRYAD 1-4

THE ECLIPTIC CONVERSATION 5-25

Psalm I 6
Antiphon I 7
Psalm II 8
Antiphon II 9
Psalm III 10
Antiphon III 11
Psalm IV 12
Antiphon IV 13
Psalm V 14
Antiphon V 15
Psalm VI 16
Antiphon VI 17
Psalm VII 18
Antiphon VII 19
Psalm VIII 20
Antiphon VIII 21
Psalm IX 22
Antiphon IX 23
Psalm X 24
Antiphon X 25

MIRROR OF NYX 27-68

Phosphokinase Ablaze 28
True Self 30
Parathesos 30
Shards Of Death 30
The Sun Sheds Its Skin 31
Rigour Mortis 32
If Any 32
The Release Of Our Souls' Doves 33
Maenad 34
Under My Skin 34

MIRROR OF NYX ....CONT...

Crimson 35
The House Of Souls 36
Avalon Ascendant 38
Confessor / Possessor 40
Siren 42
Queensryche 43
Diabolo Vampyr 44
Hope 45
The Boneyard 46
Threnody Of A Sea Nymph 48
Befallen 49
Ineffectual Cruet 50
Law of Divine Oneness 51
Falling Apart 52
Surveil 52
Discarded 53
Today My Dreams Fell Apart 54
Shards 55
Oil To Water 56
Vermillion 57
Fates Allotted Time Expired 58
Brutalised Illusion 60
Dolour 61
Consigned To Oblivion 62
Feather, Gether And Leather 64
Narcolepsy 66
Crystal Clear 67
Luna 68
Moonstone 68

THE LARGESSE OF SOLARIS 69-105

Tapestry Of Smiles..70
Labyrinth 71
Disestablished And Dignified..72
High Priestess..74
Whirlpool Of Time 75
Star's Conspiracy 76
Transmute, Transfixed, Transformed 77
Celestial 78
In This Moment 79
Cathartic Love...80
Captive 81
Moth To Flame 82
Your Scent 83
Oasis 84
Without You 85
Dream Whisperer 86
Inner Peace..87
Gypsy..88
Beats Between The Vesper 89
Contemplated Aspirations 90
The Casting Of My Chrysalis 91
Fated Beyond The Horizon..92
CAN..93
Extirpated Greenhouse 94
Reticulated Repose 95
Supercilious Solicitude..96
She Is The Night..100
Transpicuous Transgressions...101
Divine Ruination...102
Pomelo Dejection..104

GLOSSARY

DACITE, DARKNESS, AND DIVINITIES DIALOGUE

(Poetry in the mourn/morn)

I, DRYAD

Special Bonus:
A character from a fantasy novel series slowly and lovingly being created.

Angela Psalm

I, Dryad

I have a story to tell;
a tale of the beginning of me,
one filled with wonder and mysticism,
I was found near a quaint farming town,
huddled between two outstretched trees.

I was a gift upon humanities cataclysm,
some say it was strange for me to be found
on a secluded and decayed road,
some were convinced
that I was an abomination,
an evil sprite that would
steal a child's soul and with it
let hell on earth unfold.

Alas, I was but a wee child
who was much loved.
I had two amazing parents
who sacrificed it all.
In their last breath
a spell was cast;
a transference
of memories and life force.

Now in their stead
only a shell remains—
with two outstretched limbs;
our family—through vile actions—
are now splinted.

DACITE, DARKNESS, AND DIVINITIES DIALOGUE

They were both tricked into
an odyssey of disrepute;
sent out to placate the greed
of a fellow villager.
Unbeknownst to them;
the evil yet to unfold—
promised innocence
for the power foretold.

My parents, out of
the goodness of their hearts;
made haste in helping
their friend in need.
Only to find their sacrifice
would be their undoing.
They fought to save my life
from its darkest greed.

Alone, a child cries for help
to the world of light;
unknown—the special powers
they possess.

They—
not human,
nor shifter,
nor demon,
sought after celestial and
stardust shower's caress.

continued

Angela Psalm

Mother Earth watched
the child, on bended knees
and heard the mournful pleas.

Gaia sent friends
in the form of Flora and Fauna,
with a language lost
in time and reality.

Dryad of old
without the bonds of family,
sought solace amongst
fireflies and butterflies—
and their ethereal skies.

She became I—
Dryad of humankind.
To walk the earth,
a keeper of humanities truest words,
an old soul lost in;

Dragon's fires,
    Phoenix ashes
        and the Sands of Time.

This is but the Prologue of an ancient story,
the beginning of fables and fantasies,
in loves enchanting glory.

THE ECLIPTIC CONVERSATION

A chapter filled with the Psalm and Modern Voice, conversations between The moon and sun.

Angela Psalm

PSALM 1

My thought folds into incessant memories,
once spellbound in a kismet supernova.
A wonderment of things done differently;
where Clandestine became our cosmic Casanova.
As night radiates the iniquity brighter
to where sometimes the darkness stands still;
each day is plunged more into the depth—
leaving behind the insidious rain of all living things.
And... in the quiet, a single tear drops
through the roar of escalated pain.

But you have walked away without words.
You have become the stain of my disdain.
Your eyes are mirrored stars—
a synthesis of good and evil,
Solstice of the eternal sun;
a celestial is born from Hell's upheaval.
My song for you is written on the sheet of life—
within the echo of a sorrowful mourn.

We have been;
captured and enslaved in eternal design
while crawling back into Intimacy's dawn.
Please infer me into the silence of ellipses—
flail gooseflesh into brailed love notes.
Know my shadow as she speaks in eclipses,
roaring into Sentiment's path and misquotes.
We have become a cult of Love's devotees.

As star-crossed soulmates, we wear the mark—
inside a composition of broken, sacred melodies.
Fated to be a twisted in the depravity
of a Luciferian heart.

DACITE, DARKNESS, AND DIVINITIES DIALOGUE

ANTIPHON 1

We often spoke of dreams.
We often spoke of desires.
We often spoke in galvanising gleams—
igniting our wildfires.

But, now we are wordless;
our voice boxes no longer hold hope.
The love once treasured—now worthless,
we've become a soulless trope.

Ash now lines my footprints,
along the highways we had travelled.
A cinder lit from out of our misery's splints—
while our grief unraveled.

I will not rue each moment, vocalised,
even if our uttered words were articulated.
So, I hold onto the memory—
that this life, once idolised, was indeed a lesson;
that we were never fated.

Angela Psalm

PSALM 11

Born of starlight, inside a Nebulous desire,
the faceless demon beckons me into his arms;
kisses and silence frolic upon hypnotic red lips of fire—
a voiceless haunting, with his comforting psalms.

Into the embrace of a reaper's deceit;
as our fervor floats in a carnival of clouds,
where our ardor is the embodiment of liquid heat.

Like a summer seduction sunset, it leaves,
wanton hues painting promises aroused.
If I could save the world, it would start with you;
for emptiness only exists without your presence.
My cosmos' compass and my Solaris in the heavens,

You have always been my only truth.

I have been born into
a beautifully structured, selfish world;
where laid perversity in a field of love—
watching the majesty of flora in its happiness unfurl.

Enveloped in a blanket of twinkling stars above,
I found strength in the darkness, but fear lived there too.
Between her deathless diaries
their lines of loss were housed in despair;
each syllable of scripture became an elixir of dew—
an eternal life without care.

My courage shone through the sunrise—from the night of you.
Can you not hear the unspoken word?
A layered silence of a psithurism—a language of lies.

A pupae transformed into a luminescent butterfly.

Watch her wings extend...

Antiphon 11

I was born of breath and bone,
from the purest of love.
I was given the tools to live alone,
from the pieces of a shattered heart.
These eyes of mine cast the word; demented,
and I wondered why my thoughts were dark.

This old soul writhed; I was tormented.

I scribed my emotions
in a ledger like a sentimental clerk.
The tears of reaping shed,
while inside, I bled.

Surrounded by many, yet unable to connect.
Suspicion of betrayal—my only discord.
Will comfort come with time to reflect,
while letting go of my every negative thought?

Angela Psalm

PSALM III

Her ink illuminates
hues of poetic bruising;
a rainbow of seduction in
the transcendence, dear muse.
The calligraphy of a monograph
of technicolor diffusing.
Rhyme me into your every cell
where our noumenon imbues
an indelible resurrection.

Hades finds the dirge in reflections
and shadows framed in imperfections.
Clutching the sunflower of my life,
let loose, my mournful night.
In the dim light of emitting souls,
we stood as strangers, alone in the cold.

Nuanced in humanity,
our conceptual reality.
I once carried my sword on my tongue
and the shield over my heart.
A warrior-lover of your holy temple,
my love, your transcendental.

I give my life to see you smile brightly,
let me be your knight.

With her last anguished breath,
she set her empathy free—
felt her emotions sink into her depth;
a bleeding ink to revelry,
a smolder of flame,
a sentiment that reigns,
a fallen angel setting worlds on fire,
a temptress in a want of your desire.

ANTIPHON III

You are the heat that surrounds my soul.
The infinite kisses;
the desire, engulfing me whole.

Let me touch your skin
and leave behind passions braille—
eyelids shut to light,
I will be your guide;
while traversing a lost paradise's trail.

See me ablaze, while I gaze into your spirit.
Memories seared, or yet to be made.
I am overtaken with; **the you**,
every. single. minute.

I am the senses in our sensibility—
an embodiment of sensual thirst,
savored only by your vivacious vitality.

Call my name into the music
trapped inside your voice.

Let loose the imprisoned expression.

Give me hope that in the end—
I will always be your
one. true. choice.

PSALM IV

Once a tortured wreck unleashed—
watch this kintsugi-soul released.
Bathe me in the sins of your delicious lips,
and adore me in your unholy tabernacle.

While resting in your petrichor petals,
I become a ceremonially sacrificed storm.
The stratum bleeds crimson in sacrificial form—
as innocence waters the fields of cockspurs.

Masked corrupters observe as evil occurs,
harbingers oversee in dismay while reapers slay.
Long forgotten laid the pain of paresthesia,
deserted, emotional, amnesia,
a pin-pricking anesthesia.

Held in stasis, a wave
of inclination overtakes us.
As we close our eyes in numbed despair—
within an obsidian glare.
It has now become a turnstile return,
while watching my hope burn.

This evening's early eclipse over Earth's ether,
evolved into an enigmatic essence.
A celestial embodiment empowered by
an exquisite empress
of emerald-green evanescence.

Steep me in sacrificed sleepless nights
awakening dawns providence.
There the golden butterflies on lilac tulips—
roam on twilight's silence.
Awaiting upon a memory of dreams
in a field of mournful meadows.

As loud clicking wings sweep away insomnia's shadows.

DACITE, DARKNESS, AND DIVINITIES DIALOGUE

ANTIPHON IV

Lost in restless thoughts,
I stay awake in my indentured haunts.
Sleep, no longer a bedfellow,
exhausted as my anxiety taunts.

Another night of crumpled sheets
sighs escaping from the lips of frustration.
Too tired to write or keep my eyes open,
but not enough to rest in my own damnation.

Dear insomnia, give me over to rest.
For alone, my slumber seems unachievable.
Agony only lingers in REM's terrors.
Rest for this soul seems irretrievable.

No longer does this farrow sound in blankets,
nor find warm peace in the arms of dreams.
So, I must ask the barkeep for a shot of melatonin,
and breathe on apnea's slipstreams.

Angela Psalm

PSALM V

You were a supplicated endearment of forever;
the void of heartbreak, fleeting like the dawn.
Yearning to covet you into safety's endeavor,
but ruination became the bittersweet swansong.

My temperance of an empress beauty,
you are the effortless echoes of profound whispers;
who seeks sunset prisms cloaked in onyx perpetuity—
as you frolic in the garden of self-love and joyous kisses.
Dispelling cobwebs of sorrow in the fields of tomorrow,
muted words, sad lips—unheard.

I was once sustained
in an unreciprocated love of sorrow.

So, we justified our friendship
in the wistfulness transferred,
a visceral emptiness rather than
being cocooned alone.
For it is a lonely road—
without a home at the end of the rainbow.
There linger, the lines of a powerful poetry abode.

We lovingly encircle the souls
in the sacred valley of philanthropy.
Surrendering into the cadence
while embraced in serendipity.
In our linguistic battle of obeisance,
we have been leached of empathy.

Farewell to my freefall limbic chaos,
she is lost within the dance of life.
I've embraced death's cataclysmic séance,
pirouetting in all its dizzying heights;
unearthing and expunging trauma.
A dance card with your name in flight,
become a Phoenix rebirthed from the ashes of her.

Antiphon V

I knew what it was to love a fleeting moment,
an invitation of a sweet, treasured memory.
I knew I was never meant for "forever,"
or the eternal company.

I am the sum of many "I love you's,"
the rapture of happy times.
So, I have put aside the epicenter of regret
and have accepted my emotions are wholly mine.

PSALM VI

We are steeped leaves of soulful tea,
our dreams are played upon a bed of poetry.
As it soothes the heartache in me—
made by many hands, from people of distant lands.
Each word—a stepping stone.
Each piece—a living tome.

I wish to cleanse this hollow heart of mistrust
by filling my soul with stardust
while immersed in a cosmos of temperance.
I am there in faltering fantasies,
falling stars—like buried casualties.

Harrowing souls hide, and the world seeks;
I close my eyes into imagined sleep.
We are twin flames in the rain of karmic despair,
reincarnated to live in repeat
under the halo of our cosmic flair.

Two souls meant to revolve
in each other's solar system—
tortured beings tied down
in unuttered fate's wisdom.
He loves his Blue and in dreams
he delved into his depths
where her sky kisses the sea
through rainbows and sunsets.
These star-crossed lovers spend eternity
looking into each other's eyes,
such beauty, such certainty, such clarity defies.

A celestial being having travelled through time,
soul-searching the equinox paradigm,
only to realise that it was an aspiration
trapped in a loop of salvation.

DACITE, DARKNESS, AND DIVINITIES DIALOGUE

ANTIPHON VI

Mythology and Theology line my heritage.
The words between each lesson speak to me.
Time and again, I sought another chance to live,
to know that if I erred, I could amend the possibility.

Angela Psalm

PSALM VII

Oh, sweet mother Selene—
my muse of the night,
ascribe me in your iridescent light,
as you bathe me in cosmic delight—
tidal love, serene.

Surrounded by eviscerated faces, dark cavernous places,
grime embedded in nail beds of twisted fate.
Terror tremors from a triggered trauma-induced state.
Shallow breathing in an upheaval of fainting coma.
Will I find my way back
or is this a terminable—over?

If my walls could only speak—
they'd bleed, they'd reap,
but instead, they wail about your loss;
perverted savior mounted on her cross.

While she ambles in Dysphoria,
set alight, this soul in your Euphoria.

Corrupted effulgence,
an ineffable assaulted pretense,
an eclipse in twisted nature,
a depth of hell awaiting her,
a tortured solace of pain,
returning home again.

Then, Zen-like gardens arise from the behest of the Silent one,
surrounded by the warmth of his heaven's sun.

ANTIPHON VII

I ebb and move like the cycles of the moon,
spirited by all that is magic.

At times, I don't know
who is mirrored in my reflection,
or whether I am ruled by all that is traumatic.

I want to be whole and free of mental anguish.
Find strength in the things I can be.
Accepting that which I cannot control.
Delight in the happy times, and not in forgery.

I am aquatic, for I find freedom in the open sea—
the saline tides that go on
and on toward life's horizon.

Watch me shine in the hues of this universe,
and slip below the rim of sighs
as I return home.

Angela Psalm

PSALM VIII

As I return to earth
in the composition of ash and dust;
your spell has been cast.
I rise with the elements
while enveloped in life's tenements.

Engulf me in your embrace,
while we fly in the face of destiny's disgrace;
a prisoner of desire.
Salacious souls interlaced—
tied in sighs knots
where angels are the icons of gods.

I've only let go of the burden of your hate
and let go of my heart—which has been estranged.
I contained the shadows and set myself free.
Darkness, you will not touch this soul's decree.

Your carnal indulgence burns through velvet skin,
heated fields of sired pleasures, therein.
A vessel encased in Lucifer's desires—
each bolus wades through the voices of liars.

Yet you sent me postcards from Hell,
cursed and under Mephistopheles' spell.
Each night, I am bathed in your fiery prose
from our unhinged, conjured, vernacular repose.

DACITE, DARKNESS, AND DIVINITIES DIALOGUE

ANTIPHON VIII

I welcomed the sweet surrender,
the open arms to psalms.
The never-ending walk
across the cobble stones.

Watch me throw the loose change,
hear it smash the glass inside the pain.
I cannot stop what already is in motion—
that my life is coming to an end.

Cut.   *Cut.*   *Cut.*
The scissors take sharp slices into air.

I am ready and willing
for the seamstress of fate
to rip the blueprint fabric foundation.

A numberless thread unstitched estate.

Angela Psalm

PSALM IX

This proud diaphanous
silent storm chaser, battles—
once an orphaned child
castaway in a cruel world,
this enclave warrior holds death in chattels.
A sinister Reaper's castings, unfurled.

Ashes of alphabetic nuances were scattered throughout.
Tears, now evaporated and encircled with pain,
littered in burning words, once were avowed.

Liberate me—from the flames.

Feel me center your precision—
where hues were left like a dominant platitude;
amongst the paint-brushed voices of my indecision.
Large brushstrokes of loneliness
leave a residue on a canvas of pulchritude.

Muse me—mislead the form conceptually.

Moonlit midnight, hold me in your omnipresence.
Wrap your stars neatly around my scars.
Oscillate my soul into the lullaby of coalescence.
Unrestrained schemes from darkness to hopeful hearts.

If I could forget the things—people don't say,
my whispering pain would dismiss them instead.
I could close my eyes and not think of ending it that day,
tears stain the path of secrets best left unsaid.

When did we become part of this artificial existence?
That love was artifice,
when an ordinance made parents non-existent,
strangers set lambs to sacrifice.

ANTIPHON IX

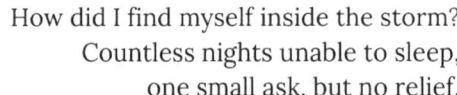

How did I find myself inside the storm?
Countless nights unable to sleep,
one small ask, but no relief.

An unmovable trauma,
a radio silence of unease,
a locksmith without keys.

But I have weathered all seasons,
reaching out for a safe harbour,
to find the jetty to self-ardour.

Angela Psalm

PSALM X

Place upon my head a daisy crown,
the sunshine chain, your luminescent smile;
threaded gold, matching soul.

I have been awoken from an ephemeral sleep,
a celestial essence igniting your desired heat.
With all your Hell in my Heaven, you have me seduced.
This Archangel seeks his Hellcat, his sensual muse.

Come, Temptress, I await thee.

A lexicon lives in veins of empathy,
vomitus in ebony poetic preservation,
a soul lost in dusk scrolls of speculation.

Existing on the edge of sanity,
look into my soul, the sentient of me.
You have stripped me of humanity's reign.
Now unbathed, I have encompassed evil's stain.

Lost in my dark world of demonic possessions,
where even the holy water evaporates in regretful confessions.
Exhaling the tenebrosity that resides within;
toxins dispel as I breathe in the sunshine, therein.
I sense when the numbness disappears—
as Pandora's Box captures my fears.

Your vile kiss is hypnotic, as this life is myopic.

You sear my soul in surrendered mercy.
I am now an enchanted burden—spelled by your beast.

DACITE, DARKNESS, AND DIVINITIES DIALOGUE

ANTIPHON X

Please send me into your complexity,
within a sizzling darkness, tattooed and etched.
Watch me customise myself inside your exclusivity,
an open arc of your breadth.

I am the lost meaning in ancient languages,
a spectral object of sensual step.
A metaphor in biblical passages,
a meagre temptation upon one's breath.

There is light and shade in the tone of your voice,
pitch-perfect in the illusion of touch.
A harmony that entraps me with little choice.
A combustible friction that can never be too much.

MIRROR OF NYX

The dark psyche of a cycle of internalised torture.

Angela Psalm

PHOSPHOKINASE ABLAZE

Winter is coming;
as I exist in a piezometer.

Perpetual veil of emotional **connection**;
an aging conduit of enzymatic **translation**.

We are a new love language
that few would understand.
Communing in a mendacious zone on **demand**,

Can you not hear the musical annotation
between the breath of each word?
The soft touch of an anatomical morse code
that flutters like a frightened hummingbird.

We are more than the endearment overused.
We are a corrupted symbol of 'I love yous'.

So, lay me down amongst
all the unconsecrated dead epistles graves,
while we swim through the sea
of our recurring memory's waves.

DACITE, DARKNESS, AND DIVINITIES DIALOGUE

You have existed in the long corridors,
inside these lifeless hearts.
Substrate and cofactor in the war
of the hemispheres
as they become the shattered parts.
I see you... although I am blind.
I hear you... through gypsy hands.
I feel you... In the vast emptiness.
In every note of your seasonal blues melody,
sing me a song dear sorrow.

For I am only home when you move me.

Angela Psalm

TRUE SELF

I am the silence between dusk and dawn.
The sweet temptation across your lips.
I am your tempo within your musical score.
Your firefly when darkness writes her hieroglyphs.

PARATHESOS

Eve welcomed rainbow dreams.
Moonlit nights, and sensual screams.

SHARDS OF DEATH

I see you my dark reflection.
A twin to light's affection.

DACITE, DARKNESS, AND DIVINITIES DIALOGUE

THE SUN SHEDS ITS SKIN

Out of my palm pain pours
over the river Styx shores.
I feel the texture of your sun-shed skin.
I hear your sacrificed sadness scream;
the last second in melancholic memory mourns.

Feel the visceral strain as plague pours.
I refuse to coalesce.
I turn from tender touch.

You are a malcontented memory march.

Yet again the tears settle—
for my melancholia memory mourns.

Every inch of you, I have memorised, my sun.
Yet yesterday yearns you.

Luna, in her reverence,
reflects radiant renewal.
Her light manifests my spiritual path,
surrendering to sorrows maelstrom.

Angela Psalm

RIGOUR MORTIS

Statue, you are so quiet;
where once you spoke,
there is no sound,
yet your silence is profound.

Statue, you are so cold;
where once there was warmth,
there is no heat,
no safety blanket henceforth.

Statue, there is no movement;
where once there was grace,
there is no life,
held stillness in death's embrace.

IF ANY

Gloaming silver-sequin astral Luna sphere.
Leviathan xenial to lustfully lovelorn atmosphere.
Suffering lit droplets of midnight dew.
In darkness her moonshine illuminates you.

DACITE, DARKNESS, AND DIVINITIES DIALOGUE

THE RELEASE OF OUR SOULS' DOVES

I savour the serenade of shadow's darkness,
that you, my Sarang, may dance with light
as I languish in the sigh of tomorrows.

Delicious memories, each a patisserie of delight.
A drive-by sweeping vile repertoire.
New beginnings midway through a chapter of pain.

A naked exchange of truth with the language of fallen stars
amongst an enthusiastic fight in all souls' dove's reign.
A spoonful of celestials sprinkled to fill the void.

Whisper me the welcomes of a mellifluous symphony,
silhouetted by the destiny of time.
She heralds the heart of winter solstice, conjoined.

My adoration is mirrored somewhere in your reflection—
the promise that somewhere we will meet in affection
as the fireflies invade my night setting ablaze the sky.

She is once again gleefully driven by echoes.
Tranquil is the beauty across the canvas of a midnight sky
before the cardinal hues of sunrise in your eyes.

There, an emotional firestorm ignites our heavens,
while we undulate on the tides inside your mind—
as our essence ascends to the cosmos,
reclaiming our blessings.

Angela Psalm

Maenad

I live between the howling cries,
descending mist and moaning lies.
Where Alphas call to their Luna's heart,
allured and adrift to the sensual craft.

Bespoken Wicca magical spells,
pulsating buds' delectable nectar dwells.
Moist feminine potions and ward,
zephyr pheromones linger toward.

In amongst the coitus rhythmic sync,
entwined in pleasure we muse, we drink.
The cries of lust in haunting sanguine divine,
I am yours; I am yours; you are mine.

Under My Skin

You are imprinted under my skin.
Your ink lodged darkness within.

DACITE, DARKNESS, AND DIVINITIES DIALOGUE

CRIMSON

Hearts howl into the darkness.

The music is heard
within the travelling wind.

Speak, and an echo will return.
Hollow is the soul within.

Where is that calling symbol,
mesmerising my being?

Full moon, my magic flute,
Pied Piper of the night.

I seek the sweet temptation on my lips
as I taste the drink of the gods.

My enslavement, my curse.
I am walking death, I haunt their dreams.
I am the purveyor of mortal screams.

Angela Psalm

THE HOUSE OF SOULS

The house was old,
but it was now becoming our home.
Each night at 2 a.m. I hear what sounds like a chair fall.
Tap.Tap.Tap.

I switch on the lamp,
but everything is as it was before.
This continues to occur night after night.
Tap.Tap.Tap.

Sleep has evaded me,
my nerves are shaken, and in constant fright.
Another night, another visit from insomnia.
Tap.Tap.Tap.

So, I delve,
into the history of our home,
When I come across
a clipping of something undisclosed.
Tap.Tap.Tap.

In my very room,
the son of the previous owner,
decided to silence
the noise in his head with a rope.
Tap.Tap.Tap.

DACITE, DARKNESS, AND DIVINITIES DIALOGUE

So next,
I shopped for a smudge stick
to clear the unrest.
To allow the spirit
to move on to the next.
Tap.Tap.Tap.

I woke up again,
and I looked to the corner of the room.
My arms were full of goosebumps;
there he sat, rapping his knuckles.
Tap.Tap.Tap.

Without his lips moving,
I heard his voice in my head.
***I was trapped in a loop spell,
reliving the action of my death.***
Tap.Tap.Tap.

He moved swiftly to my side
when a scream escaped my lips.
***Now, it is your turn to die,
and join us in our house of mist.***
Tap.Tap.Tap.

Angela Psalm

Avalon Ascendant

Raised with regal steed
and innocence entwined.
Yet, I was dimmed by masculinities'
perverse divertissement.
A shadowed Phoenix akin
to dragons and hidden by sorcery.

My name is Morgana—
once whispered in adoration,
now a fearful lament,
dependent on which cautionary tale
you wish to take heed;
a powerful woman from healer to villain or queen.
Stories are often told from the victor's perspective.
I was branded with the scarlet letter
and wickedness ran through me.

DACITE, DARKNESS, AND DIVINITIES DIALOGUE

My despondent heart's inclination,
was for only one intendant.
He is now long-buried,
and still, I grieve;
still yearning my Beltane reprieve.
When days are long,
the world's weight conjures
the mists to wear thin.

I call to you, my lover beyond
the mortal coil, and you call to me.

Candle burn bright, burn fire,
keep within your desire.
Listen to the words I speak,
clear the path to what I seek.
Let my wishes all come true,
as they burn this night with you.

Upon the incantation the dissipating mist from
Avalon's curtain welcome's you home.

Angela Psalm

CONFESSOR / POSSESSOR

Frayed—
Broken—
a stutter unspoken.
My features of fragmentation.

Hollowed—
Depressed—
adrift in emptiness.
Souls lamenting perfection.

Devastation—
Procrastination—
unbridled pain awoken.
Segmented pain realisation.

Neurotrauma—
Emotional coma—
scarred in your stress.
Fractured under duress.

Exhalation—
A Zen like pose.
An angelic spirit arose.
Bowed over vents as celestials descend.

DACITE, DARKNESS, AND DIVINITIES DIALOGUE

Pirouetting—
Dancing in forgetting,
a conjoint saint and sinners wedding.
Shaded linear bookends.

Shadows—
Transcendence—
haloed luminescence.
Star shower omnipresence.

Levitating—
Gods traverse—
a corrupted universe.
Evil bends, righteousness reinvents.

Spin, spin little seduction,
gossamer webbed essence.
Stalled in post-production,
torpidity in somnolence.

Angela Psalm

SIREN

That day I threw away the key,
in a drunken haze of rage.
Destroyed by you—I lay on the floor.

I ask myself, How did our love turn to hate?
One day turned into two,
two days melted into a week,
a week became a month.

A month lost without the algorithm to speak.

Not to you,
not to my family or friends—
I could not even face myself.
My looking glass was shattered
from the lucid ambiance of heart's end.

I cried until I could no more.
I stared at the empty space
where my heart once was.
Then I slept my life away,
cast myself into a soulless pit.
A sequence of loss.

Then, my spirit finally climbed out,
and with a little courage I reached for help.
The pain clutched to the depths.
I am hoping this is the end of my hell.

You claimed my essence under a spell,
but I will not allow love to be a weakness.
You were just undeserving of me,
I will never fear that which is endless.

Let the darkness you cast upon me,
burn... burn... and cleanse away the impure.
For I will continue to believe,
in the magic of happiness,
and not be tempted by your Siren's allure.

DACITE, DARKNESS, AND DIVINITIES DIALOGUE

QUEENSRYCHE

I am a heaving ruse from tormented agony,
reflective seasons stare back at me.
A march onto a kingdom within a false decree.
A coveted land of Queendom set to rise.
Goddess caressed province, a saviour in disguise.
Below, she stands with the strength of Hercules,
a sapphire sky blankets her skin to appease.
She refuses to live as a slave to tradition.
A pawn to her forefathers in negotiated diction.
She watches a face of vigilance that could belong to me.
A chimerical view and yearning,
as it is returning to the unjaded nominee.
Upon contemplation within the musical sound of signs,
musing, and rumination; something inside her dies.

My anchoress conveys
the vestal of culpability in delinquency.
A repentance, in a feeling of compunction to be free.

Dear sister, please forgive me for I sanctioned in concede,
the punishment that originally belonged to me.
A betrothal of pain, to a man that showed love
through his violated blade.

So, she looked upon the instrument of her torture,
admonishing it to her sister's face.
The beginning of her overture.
Here she recited what the oracle did not foresee,
the peroration of vitality deceased in discourtesy.

Angela Psalm

DIABOLO VAMPYR

Amongst the howling cries,
my garden grows as far as one can see.
Pinwheels littered with lies
yielding moving in perfect musical harmony.

While I in daylight slumber—
sweet ambrosia is supple to my lips.
My lover whimpers on my dragon's breath
while the prey prays within the hunter's keep.

For crimson runs free menu de jour.
Like a peacock spider's mesmerising dance,
I lull the condemned to inveracity.
My ivory takes to your carotid neuro trance.

While I hold to blissful silence a heartbeat away,
pulsating through obtained matter.
This monster hides within the shadows,
carving up humanity like a buffet platter.

DACITE, DARKNESS, AND DIVINITIES DIALOGUE

HOPE

Today another human suit,
in the role predetermined for my gender.
Only I see the real me,
when I gaze inside my pain-filled decanter.
The matrix of complexity,
I walk blindly into the maze.
The surface does not match the depth,
I see no ending to the cultural haze.

Angela Psalm

THE BONEYARD

Our ship was captured by Poseidon's fury.
He was much in ire as he discovered the loss
of his most beloved treasure.
I stayed steadfast into the course of a new shore.

Then the ship shuddered,
her body cracked and popped,
like the sound of subluxation.
That is when I lost balance and
the bronze band fell into the sea.

Damn it—

Now I have become your salvation.
I plummeted the course of the ring.
Into the storm swirled murky water I followed,
as my love sank towards the ocean's floor.

Her soul was bound to what seemed like a trinket,
cursed to live her days touching my skin,
and I—wanting more.

Sometimes in the darkest moments,
we are not lost but found among
moonbeams of twilight.
The catacomb's spirit
within our heart will find its way.
I will not let go of hope, **my love,**
that we shall meet once again.

DACITE, DARKNESS, AND DIVINITIES DIALOGUE

As I sink deeper in the waters close to Tartarus,
I transform into my true self—Proteus.
Psamathe, my wife kidnapped,
and then imprisoned—
she would not give in to Poseidon's lust.

The betrayal of my lord was unfathomed—
what inconceivable idea in that twisted soul,
did he think that I would gift him my wife?

Finally, the ring in my grasp,
I teleported swiftly to shore.
I could not tempt my own fate,
while the God of the Sea
hunted the likes of me.

As I stood looking back,
I said farewell to home forever more.
If I stepped back into salinity,
my death would be all that I would foresee.

Sometimes in the darkest moments,
we are not lost but found
Among the twilight,
the ossuary within our heart
I will defend against
the treacheries boneyard
in hopes destined plight.

Angela Psalm

THRENODY OF A SEA NYMPH

In the depths of the sea,
no one will see these tears.
Silently she thinks in haunting pleasure.
No lighthouse shine could take away
from your lilac gaze.

When you fell into troubled waters to escape—
I was bereft.

In you, I once had my home
nestled in the heart of your eyes.
We allowed misguided words and tumultuous waves—
they crashed against a sail without a name.

For the nameless carry the burden of deep dark sin.
Emotionless—devoid of any connection, they drift away.
Uncharted briny that won't cleanse the stain therein.

An unfamiliar spanner in my chest silenced my cold heart.
Like old, rusted cogs they scrape painfully but do not start.
The haunting pleasure of pain for a water sprite.
Love is love but not always will it embody
rainbow hues of delight.

While happiness straddles the bodice of despair,
each movement—a displeasure of nothingness;
in the suffocating light of solemnity, it wanes.

As her body descends to the floor, her last thoughts are:
How death seems the only answer to apathy and benignity.

DACITE, DARKNESS, AND DIVINITIES DIALOGUE

BEFALLEN

No purity is on demand
at the horror of your hand.
No angelic remnants left,
only the stained angel wings cleft.

I wear the scars of their weight on my soul.
I have been sliced away like a filet mignon.

Daddy dearest you can go to Hell!

I have been created from your demonic self.
I no longer want to ascend to your side.
Let my befallen and forsaken self-disqualify.

Here, take the symbols that you abhorrently detest,
as I continue to torture myself with the poison I ingest.

Angela Psalm

INEFFECTUAL CRUET

Encapsulated glass.
A decanted encampment,
left empty the jars.
Only a vacuous space,
a silent scream impasse.
An exenterated cavity
of broken hearts.

A pickled portion
of eviscerated offal.
Bathed in the healing
innocence of unicorn tears.
As it consumes the corruption
of the unlawful.
The vindictive violence of fateful fears.

So many words,
so many feet have walked abroad.
An action far from any reaction.
A cosmos of plucked satellite stars.
Inanimate statues.
In the raptures of déjà vu.
The repeated I owe yous.
Where only the righteous can dine.
A clearance of inaction and the inaudible blues.

The subtle I love yous.
The rues, the regrets.
The list of things unchecked.
My once true glory.
You're my unfinished story.

DACITE, DARKNESS, AND DIVINITIES DIALOGUE

LAW OF DIVINE ONENESS

One plus—
one... that divides into half.
Half of a wholeness,
no divination is profound.
When it comes,
to the realism of darkness.

Damn, that silence of sound.
Resounding an echo,
in the way of nothingness.
Our definition of darkness.

You are a blessing.
Blessed that death is near.
For she wages your rage.
A wrapped Reaper of darkness.

No life to engage.
Encrusted by the corpse.
For she can be no more.
Reality is darkness.

Let darkness be the key to your celestine door.

Angela Psalm

FALLING APART

How does it feel to fall apart?

When you lie to everyone,
with delusion and grandeur.
By separating your ego,
including that part of yourself
you have kept locked away.

When your soul no longer inhabits
the shell that is left behind.
When your life is full of self-loathing.
When the smile hides the pain, the tears,
and the chasm in your heart.

If this is how it feels to fall apart—
then I am there—falling into decay.
No tender hands entwined.

SURVEIL

You are the dirge of monochromatic sepulchre.
The profound eyes that whisper death.
My paralleled superstition to my lucky charm.
The embouchure of harmonic breath.

DACITE, DARKNESS, AND DIVINITIES DIALOGUE

DISCARDED

The wind picks up the note,
last discarded by a lover's quarrel.
She ambles through the air,
leaving the bitter taste of sorrel.

The words written on her surface
were a small reminder
of the pain and burden she carried.

Higher and Higher,
each horizon another memory—
torn pages from happier times.
As every minute passes it evaporates,
and the sun—no longer shines.

The weight of sorrow
eventually becomes too hard to bear.
Laden with all the screams
and shouts and pain.

She lost her fight for flight,
and came tumbling down
like a meteor without an orbit plane.

As her Universe no longer existed,
a black hole opened and consumed
all that was good in her life.

So now she ambles once again.
Her treasures, they gather dust
amongst the detritus denied.

Angela Psalm

TODAY, MY DREAMS FELL APART

I am surrounded by faces, voices, and love.
I hear the discourse and feel the lovely chaotic embraces.
But, the voices are distant and to the touch I am numb.
I am immersed in a world that only sees the shell.

Thousands of souls who take to word,
and yet, I wandered lonely as a cloud.
I am the void between the empty spaces,
where dreams are buried to be faded memories.

My soul's diaphanous on connection,
but heavy on mournful graces.
I am climbing under fateful skies and long goodbyes.
Parched and starved of stars sacrificed for a wish,
but I will hope against the torrent wind of blatant lies.

DACITE, DARKNESS, AND DIVINITIES DIALOGUE

SHARDS

I am trapped within the beam of the silver moon.
Clearly, the glass ceiling must be held to account.
Caged by your unending unscrupulous doom.
Again, I am pushed to the edge of what is paramount.

Your locutions are like shards of cold ice,
penetrating the moments of promised perfidy—
scraping and inducing scars to my demise.

My wounds unfurled and untethered taciturnity.

Angela Psalm

OIL TO WATER

I want to take a blunt scabbard—
theatrically slice it across my chest.
So, I may cut my heart out and deaden my synapses—
as the sound of it beating hurts too much.

To not feel.
To not love.
To allow the coagulation of pain in all chambers.
To stop my heart from breaking
into minuscule pieces.
Willing it—to bleed out and welcome death.

All my dreams began and ended with you.
Now a photograph in time—as it fades so does my hope.
Lost vitality that I will never recover.
Your lips—I shall never feel again.
Your perfume—I shall never savour.
Your words—whispered in my ear.
Your fingertips—across my skin.

I was foolish to believe I was everything you needed.

I hope to say goodbye,
but you are never here.
I hoped that the end was a lie.

Narcissus's pond illuminates.

The void was enough to know…
It was time to let you go.

DACITE, DARKNESS, AND DIVINITIES DIALOGUE

VERMILLION

I shut the door behind me,
trapped between life and death.
I took the blade to remove
the encompassing feeling,
bringing forth numbness out of its depth.
Instead, I cut my wrists,
across the cephalic.

I watched my pain pour out.

As my soul tremors all the way through—
I hear a knock at the door.

It echoes.

I ignored that knock.
Hoped it would go away.
I lay floating in crimson water.
Then, I hear the door slam open
into the corridor of dreadful cries.

From afar, I hear flute tunes—
sirens of a second chance.

This was never a decision made lightly.

Overwhelmed, in a feeling of disgust:
so dirty, so unclean, such revulsion.
All innocence, gone, and no one to trust.

My humanity was ripped away,
"From family, with love,"
promised I was their princess,
while ravaged, and left in the dark.

Angela Psalm

FATES ALLOTTED TIME EXPIRED

Tonight is my last night on Earth.
My prayers were unanswered.
The Doctor gave me less than 3 months to live.
This body is slowly decaying, my answer to cancer.

My chauffeuring days are almost over,
and I step into my car for the last time.
Soon, I will clock out from work, and
figuratively, with my life.
It will be my end, my choice.
Is it weird that I am excited and
my spirit is soaring high?

I greet my last client
and chills run down my spine.
Our destination is The Underworld Pass.
So uncanny, that this would be my last ride.
My client says, **Firstly, I need to collect my family
if you don't mind.**

I start to cough and cover my mouth
with a handkerchief.
I see crimson splatter
and the pain spreads throughout my chest.

Thanatos introduces himself.
I begin to feel better,
as I drive to The Underworld Pass—
where the streets align with death.

DACITE, DARKNESS, AND DIVINITIES DIALOGUE

Thanatos signaled for me to stop here.
There was naught a creature in sight.
The door opens
and two other passengers climb in.
First, a beauty with a bright light of clarity
and a dazzling smile.
This is Nyx, my mother.

Then Hypnos climbs in
with dreamlike eyes.
Thanatos instructs me
to keep my eyes ahead
for my own good.
Hypnos has a knack
to entice and mesmerise.

Tonight, the fates allotted time expires.

Then Thanatos laid his hand on my shoulder,
**Father, it is time for you
to let go of your human shell.**

I turn to Thanatos,
who was encased with
darkness and strength.
The beauty I have longed for, smiles—
and opens the Gates to Inferno,
and our home sweet home, Hell.

Angela Psalm

BRUTALISED ILLUSION

I woke only to find that everything was just an illusion.
It's the line I feed myself every time I awake to this.
The smell of stale nicotine in the air,
and the violation of you seeping down my legs.

A commodity sold by those who loved me.
A child bred to be brutalised in care.
A toy for the deprived in pleasure.
A bauble of pain in all its measure.

I know my time is at an end.
This resource closer to her use-by date.
So each night I close my eyes and I dream
that I lived only for a moment's nightmare.

But I awakened again in a different bed.
The smell of stale nicotine in the air,
and someone else's seed between my legs.
The throbbing pain of something that does not belong there.

Tonight, I am left alone, allowed to find my own way.
A chance to dream in my meditative, watery, safe place.
I can still smell stale nicotine in the air—no seed, but peace.
This night, I don't awaken to any illusion; only darkness erased.

Restrained by walls no angel could climb.
My soul wants it all—shimmering and sublime.
So, I take my horns and pitchfork under the veil of obsidian,
where I stare you down—
for no one will destroy who I am inside.

DACITE, DARKNESS, AND DIVINITIES DIALOGUE

DOLOUR

I never thought that I'd find myself here again.
The last time I was in this very space, I hurt.
The scars are written across my soul like braille.
To the naked eye invisible
but the dolour is submersed.

I can only show happiness,
when you are the centre of its joy.
Then you push the knife deep,
your jealousy's schizophrenic psychosis,
shows its ugliness—a disfigured Creep.

My forever hurts me again.
I feel broken and immersed,
in his cursed embrace.
I found a man who loves me,
as much as he owns me.

His push and pull unravelling,
the stitch and replacing it with hate.
As much as I love you, I fucking hate you.

I hate that I allow you to make me feel the way I do.
On the surface—I look so controlled with smiles.
But underneath—I am a whimpering mess for you.

My forever hurts me as I force my lungs to work.
Inhale, Exhale, and my breath becomes laboured.
As the vapour of your poison fills my cellular self.
The stillness of midnight welcomes my death.

Angela Psalm

CONSIGNED TO OBLIVION

Father Time eats in vain where there is hope.
Maligned towers line the edge of my pitiful world.
Tempests—their impetus fury lashes upon my soul.

Digging deep with emotions unfurled,
I bathed in Heaven's kingdom by the sea—
yet, I could not spell away the stench of loss and death.
Deep into the pool of your liquid eyes, I stare—
I was lost and drowning, unable to take breath.
Chasing caterwauling calls into the depths of darkness,
loneliness is captured when misery is manifold,
and I am no longer me.
Nevermore...

An atmosphere of sorrow
does not help this soul's scar to heal.
You have wrapped me with an empathetic blanket,
like a Valkyrie's shield across the heart.
As I descend into the maelstrom, I face Fear,
and its mask no longer hides its malicious smile.
I loved alone—as the god of many faces was never you;
and this love was built on denial.
Nevermore...

DACITE, DARKNESS, AND DIVINITIES DIALOGUE

My quivering wings extended and healed
after the fractured fall from grace.
Afraid to open my love-haunted heart,
which is scarred and imperfectly laced.
I am a weary, wayworn wanderer; my path adorned
underfoot with crimson rose petals in disrepair.
Highlighted by the mystic moon's glow—
my pale skin, translucent, and a halo adorns my hair.
Nevermore...

A memory, like a shadow, casts depth,
cuts deep, and is never consigned to oblivion.
My heart was volcanic, its searing liquid
had left behind the devastation of my dominion.
With it, was the perpetual horror
of losing the chambers of my soul.
Delirium sets in, and instead
of running from all the chaos,
I embrace the screams as my opus.
Nevermore... I abhor... Nevermore...

Angela Psalm

FEATHER, GETHER AND LEATHER

I am born of green,
cocooned—
    and set to flight.
My life is long forgotten,
and so I rise, a single cell
combustion,
I ignite—
I am the imposter
    in your garden of night.
Reality is short,
    yet full of flowers.
My days are only hours.
A trickster of syndrome.
in our sky.
    I traverse alone,
ablaze of sun—
    I vanish into the numb.

DACITE, DARKNESS, AND DIVINITIES DIALOGUE

I have reached—
into the vastness.
Amnesia is relentless—
the height within the lie.
These Avarians
no longer glide.
Watch me fall.
Watch me fall
headfirst into
the mouth of a gator.
Sharp teeth,
engorging me whole.
Luminescence takes its toll.
Feed me deception.
Drowning while you
take me down
into the depths
of your boneyard.

I am bound
as I swell,
I cannot tell.
Ballooned.
Marooned.
Tethered to boulder.
A skinned-skeleton soldier.
I am only resourced.
Another art piece,
scaled in remorse.

*Let Me Go,
As I Become The
Unknown.*

Angela Psalm

Narcolepsy

In the hour
of Morpheus's awakening,
her eyes searched
in a dreamlike gaze.
Under the surface,
she sought the forsaking,
missing the boat towards
the Tartarus Maze.
Down in flames
her universal
lighthouse burns.
Doused in darkened rifts
and unfeeling waves.

Nyx crashes against the
law of her restive returns—
there she apnoea-slumbers
in sonal caves.
As she dozes
in her lullaby chambers,
she births the child that
becomes the Sandman.
Awakening the embodiment
of Ajna as she labours,
she breathes life into
the 7 pulses of command.

DACITE, DARKNESS, AND DIVINITIES DIALOGUE

CRYSTAL CLEAR

Are these new beginnings or old joys?
Or are we revisiting something
we should have left behind—
a past where it snowed for you,
stormed for me.

The tempest's fates became aligned—
the icicles danced along
the frozen lake made of tears
that belonged to us.

Within Kronos' scriptures
predictions were made that,
this too shall come to pass.

An emerald glow painted the sky—
a signal cast out to bring an end
to the darkness in La Luna's graciousness.

The moon's silvery shimmer coated me,
like a cloak guiding my lost soul
home amongst a joyous memory.

Angela Psalm

LUNA

Selene mistress of the night,
I hear your music play your notes forlorn,
your lover lives where you cannot be—
your gracious heart is torn.

The tide ebbs and flows,
symbolising your emotional throw.
Goddess with so much power,
yet, loss surrounds you at every hour.

In the darkness, you are revered,
you are the guiding light on a traveler's path,
worshipped from ancient times—
but, not even you can detain the tempest's wrath.

MOONSTONE

Opalescent goddess,
you are throne of mysticism,
and within your heart a talisman.

Your ethereal Moonstone sits high in the sky.

THE LARGESSE OF SOLARIS

Hope and light, the passage of acceptance.

Angela Psalm

TAPESTRY OF SMILES

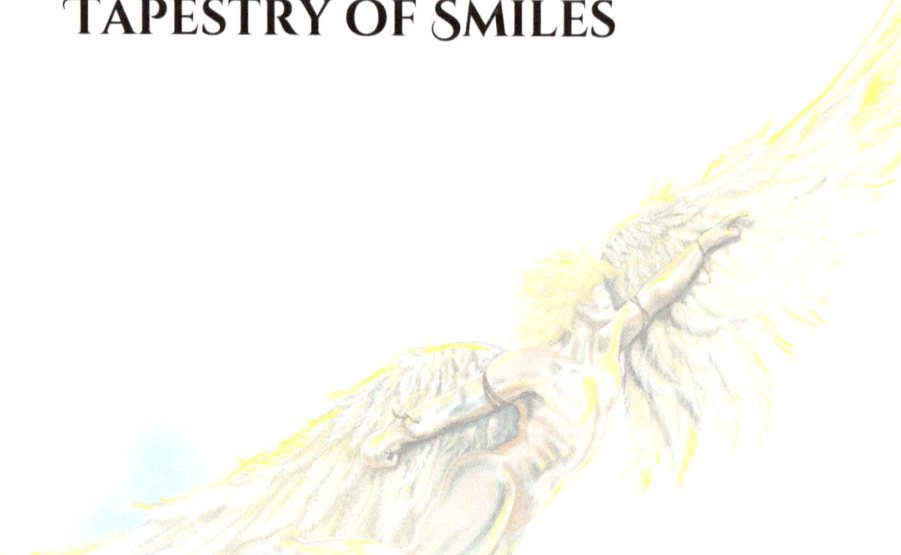

She is the embodiment of love,
mesmerised in the enchanting halo glow.

In her fragility and vulnerability, there is strength.

Love is she, a Siren, seeking her soul's overture.

Exquisitely she sings serenity in her magnum oeuvre.

DACITE, DARKNESS, AND DIVINITIES DIALOGUE

LABYRINTH

Between the silences of my day,
traversing over time,
and through the labyrinth of life,
the bones of hope hold on—
even though there are scars
stitched across my soul.
As I count my blessings,
bathed in light,
I have been weaving through
varying levels of existence.

A time-lord, celestial being
who is contained in stardust,
I move in different forms
unlocking unknown realities.
The search is in hope of you:
to find the pieces of your soul
set adrift in time—
fractured due to my selfish
and displeasing actions.

So yes, I bare the scars
across my timeless soul,
but it is you, Hope,
that I am blessed to know.
My guiding light.

Angela Psalm

DISESTABLISHED AND DIGNIFIED

For so long, I dreamt and planned.
The ifs and maybes dragged me along.
Now my dreams crash and burn,
and my ifs and maybes are gone.

How do I drag this hollow shell
that howls at the moon and the darkness in Hell?
How can I glue this shattered glass
when there is no beginning to the pain in my heart?

Where does the horizon begin or end?
When does the numbness stop and the pain begin?
I want to feel. I want to put this moment in my past.
I am not sure how long I will survive
in the numbed void within.

DACITE, DARKNESS, AND DIVINITIES DIALOGUE

I could be angry with myself
for allowing you that power,
but I accept that sacrifice is vulnerability—
in love, and life.

I will not let you take away
the happiness of *what could be.*
Now is my time to embrace
my scars and emotional fight.
To take the hollow shell of the ifs and maybes.

This phoenix has been born from the ashes—
of all that was *never to be.*

Take your selfish, ruthless, and dark heart.

I am the writer of this story, my life.

A new book is ready to be written—
a volume of happiness for me.

Angela Psalm

High Priestess

Gaia, high priestess to my soul's temple,
I seek your guidance, elemental.
You represent the head of all enchantment.
Can you foresee my desire's disbandment?

Most divine mistress, identified within your Shekhinah,
in royal blue robes and a lunar crescent heart.
Your soul is gilded in mystery and passivity,
It is time to retreat and reflect upon your world in me.

Daughter, trust your inner instincts
to guide you through the catacombs.
Your hidden talents: Intuition, Mystery,
Spiritual insight, therein looms.
Slowly unfolding, your persona reveals,
you are the water, moon—
warrior amongst life's minefields.

DACITE, DARKNESS, AND DIVINITIES DIALOGUE

WHIRLPOOL OF TIME

I returned to my own existence...
Yet, the deep pool in time draws me in.
My heart belongs in steps yet travelled...
For I have stayed to avoid Fate's string.

When I miss or long for your face,
I reach for the enchanted looking-glass.
There, my heart stands in a ripple of time.

As I yearn for future's plan to be unmasked,
do not be swayed by unfathomable skylines
or the unplanned destination of tomorrows.

Memories can be locked in a capsule of time,
buried deep in our mortal coil of sorrows.

Angela Psalm

STAR'S CONSPIRACY

I am searching through the Universal Sea,
through the Milky Way,
while languishing on Ursa Minor—
on an elliptical orbit, set free.

I am a binary star without a center.

These eyes are tired from eons of loneliness,
on fallen stars and conspiracies reflection.
Dejected and vile intergalactic theories,
sorting companionship, and adulation.
Look deep into my reflective pools.
Let me show you a constellational supernova,

Hold fast, your bountiful jewels,
while I worship you over and over.

DACITE, DARKNESS, AND DIVINITIES DIALOGUE

TRANSMUTE, TRANSFIXED, TRANSFORMED

Beloved, I sent you a letter post-haste—
when I knew I was not long for this world.
I know I had not made amends,
when I left you without a word.

Beloved, if you could hear me,
I tried to be the shell of a man.
I tried, but all I could see and feel was her—was me.
I tried to send you a letter,
but the pain was littered on the floor.

Beloved, we shared our childhood milestones—
lived our youth with reckless abandonment.
We lived and stumbled in darkness, engulfed in sorrow—
lived without you, my one guiding light.

Beloved, I transformed from a caterpillar to a butterfly.
I found the peace I sought.
I found the missing piece of our equation.
I hope you found yours.

You have never been an afterthought.

Angela Psalm

CELESTIAL

My angelic aura scans the heavens—
from the limitless energy within my core.
Helping to protect my fragile heart,
and avoiding the damage from before.

The shell I grow is impenetrable,
as I emit through Galaxy's pure love.
I search for a kintsugi-kindred soul,
to help me fill the void above.

A Millennia alone floating in vast space,
loneliness, my only companion.
Uncomfortable, unnecessary, a discarded embrace.
I want to bathe in love's glorious haze.

DACITE, DARKNESS, AND DIVINITIES DIALOGUE

IN THIS MOMENT

I needed this moment
to lie down on the lawn.
To immerse myself in the flowering aromas,
Vitamin D, happiness, and The Sun.

The bees are buzzing,
the birds are singing tunes—
Spring envelopes me in all her glory,
diffusing a transference of beautiful hues.

In this moment—
it banishes the sadness of yesterday.
I am now in a place of peace.

Let me enjoy this moment, this day.

Angela Psalm

CATHARTIC LOVE

When the world falls away,
and the most perfect moment happens.
As the sky transcends blue
and the sunshine is love, imbued.

This can only happen when trauma fades.
When the scars we share turn a pearly white.
When I sit between the space of life's lessons,
after saving me from its darkest transgressions.

Dare I say that I dream of you,
your smile singular, is exquisite.
Those lips I've wished to worship,
and the body that belongs with them.

Do you think of me when I am not there,
along those silent moments we share?
I stand close to feel your radiating fervour,
while I pretend, I do not know you're nearby.

I want to fill those empty cavities,
with only treasured memories.
You have saved this little sparrow,
and burned the pages of my darkest hour.

DACITE, DARKNESS, AND DIVINITIES DIALOGUE

CAPTIVE

I am a modern-day slave with many kinks.
My body—a temple for you to worship with your lips.
Here, on the floor, stretched out like a map to explore.
When captive, felt sublime, and you Dear M, I adore.
Here I serve you the signed contract of my own, free will,
while we ride the precipice of erotic knife's edge.
Cold steel balanced to pleasure along voyeuristic thrill.
Your thumb slowly slides across my labium superius oris—
sealed acceptance of your message.

Angela Psalm

Moth to Flame

I am a moth to flame, lost in your grace,
vulnerable to the attractive newcomer.
How did you manage to switch a dominant personality?
I was never one to fall for the relapses of other women.
I was strong, domineering, a shark in deep water;
I knew what I wanted and devoured every delicious treat.
But, in your eyes, I felt as though I was a lost little girl.

What made you so special?
What in you made me submit?

You moved slowly, circumnavigating me.
As you passed me, your breath hitched, and my heart raced.
But your force was strong and did not relent.
I was your clay to be molded for all your needs and expectations.

DACITE, DARKNESS, AND DIVINITIES DIALOGUE

YOUR SCENT

The flames ignite the scent of you.
Sandalwood permeates the evocative and exotic.
Rose on your skin as it touches mine, becomes restorative.
Menthol on your breath cools the heat you bring forth.
Tobacco touches mysteries upon kissing your lips.

Angela Psalm

OASIS

I dreamt of you last night—
at least, it felt like you.
We were sitting high up in the mountains,
with the hot sun shining through.

I felt your lips on my neck,
and your hands—exploring me.
An audible sigh then left my lips,
I've never felt so much need.

Then, you sang a haunting song,
and tears rolled down my cheeks.
I laid back into your chest as you held me.

This here, is what my soul seeks.

I am afraid to turn around,
scared this was all a mirage.
I want to continue to hear your song,
your lament—
the one that fills and breaks my heart.

DACITE, DARKNESS, AND DIVINITIES DIALOGUE

WITHOUT YOU

Phoenix, you have set fire to my world,
creating an all-consuming inferno.
Ashes float amongst the tree branches of life.
Trauma's memories, once deep-rooted,
have gone up in flames tonight.
My life, your life, is no more,
This is *our* life.
With strength, we persist.
For I have been renewed
by your healing flame.

Without you, I would not exist.

Angela Psalm

DREAM WHISPERER

How many tears have you held for me,
while watching my dreams turn to darkness?
Where whispers of a lover's breath,
caress my lips in the throws of love.
Downy parcels of Elysium comfort,
ecstasy surrounding my cranial sphere—
while you bend and change.

You reshape your soul into me,
with promises of love and hope.
Idealistic thoughts traverse my mind,
lingering through divinity's gold mine.
Blessed are my thoughts encompassing you,
as you welcome me into Heaven's truth.

DACITE, DARKNESS, AND DIVINITIES DIALOGUE

INNER PEACE

I reconcile my past,
understanding the damage
that birthed my strength.
That hurt—opened my heart,
giving me the bravery to seek love again.

Each blow—a step closer.
Each barrier—a level of understanding.
Each obstacle—a lesson learned.
Each journey—a better self.

With hate or revenge,
only darkness can be sought.
I've let go of all that anger,
I did not want to lose my soul.

I worked on myself,
and learned to love *me* once again.
I was contented with the new direction,
through letting go.

Angela Psalm

GYPSY

I have travelled into darkness,
sought solace amongst the grief;
wandered so far and wide,
like an ambling autumn leaf.

I have felt the loss,
I have dug deep into my soul—
enjoyed comfort in the emptiness,
as well as solitude on the moor.

There have been times of struggle,
but enriched in other ways,
I have never felt regret,
in all my living days.

DACITE, DARKNESS, AND DIVINITIES DIALOGUE

BEATS BETWEEN THE VESPER

We travel to seek adventure,
interconnecting with the world
and the people around us.

We roam to unknown shores
while following our dreams.
Sunrise, beaches, laughter, parties,
success, excess nonetheless.

The gloaming is where
our heart's sit dormant
between our memories
and the reveries.

They are so unlike elsewhere,
as I sigh between
sunsets, twilights, and moonbeams.

Angela Psalm

CONTEMPLATED ASPIRATIONS

Each spirit—a twinkle inside a night sky,
like sprinkles of hundreds and thousands;
a decoration of sugary delight.

Amongst my dreams and everlasting horizons,
I felt that overwhelming happiness—
like a child let loose in a candy store,
running through a field of sunflowers,
or tobogganing down a steep slope.

Do I dare to dream higher
than the stratosphere,
or plant a thought
and watch it grow?

I want to be lost in your today,
and in all things good that come my way.
Leap headfirst into the gifted,
refulgent spirit, orator of life's creations.

Efficacy of dreams to one's prayer,
aspires in a loving embrace of narrations.
A structured macarism to all readers.
A sidereal constellation of emotions.

DACITE, DARKNESS, AND DIVINITIES DIALOGUE

THE CASTING OF MY CHRYSALIS

I was a different person a year ago,
my younger self, a pupae in the lifecycle of my world.
Now, as an adult with new aspirations,
and an understanding of who I am.
I have spread my wings of multi-coloured hues
and have expanded to new horizons.

*I am no Icarus ascending to the sun,
I have a fortitude where he had none.*

This proclamation imbues—
the beginning to the end of my old self,
I have found joy in letting go of my past.

Angela Psalm

FATED BEYOND THE HORIZON

Meet me beyond the horizon,
where all concerns disappear.
Meet me beyond the horizon,
hold my hand—don't live in fear.

Meet me beyond the horizon,
where broken hearts go to die.
Meet me beyond the horizon,
for that one last goodbye.

Meet me in the next life,
as a day without you is unfathomable.
Meet me in the next life,
where humanity is charitable.

Please promise me in the next life,
that *us* won't spell a dying light.
Give me faith that this sacrifice
was not an artifice of the night.

DACITE, DARKNESS, AND DIVINITIES DIALOGUE

CAN

When darkness descends,
I know I have the light with you.
When others fall apart,
you are my glue.

When the earth trembles,
I do too—as you excite this soul.
When sadness touches humanity,
you are my sunshine whole.

When all seems lost,
with you I am found.
When the rain does not stop,
my fire roars abound.

When actions are crazy,
you are my calm atoned.
When I have no one,
you remind me—that I am not alone.

Angela Psalm

EXTIRPATED GREENHOUSE

I have long since removed
the fragmented glass—
lodged in the derma greenhouse
of scattered dreams.
There is no expanse in time
for flowers to bloom.
This here—
> **has turned from a hallowed space,**
> **only to become a hollowed room.**

I have long been
the dhurrie laid upon
prickling petals of a long
forgotten heirloom.
This life was once a visage
of sunflowers
but now a hyacinth of misery.

And, I cannot kneel in prayer
for I am surrounded
by the blood and bone of your lies.
Incarcerating me
in the dark dwelling...
reaping from a chorus of cries.
I have learned to exist
in the abyss of lost warmth,
the chilling pool
of arctic sunshine.
I am the last languishing
orchid you left behind.
No sun will ever rise again,
while hope withers and dies.

DACITE, DARKNESS, AND DIVINITIES DIALOGUE

RETICULATED REPOSE

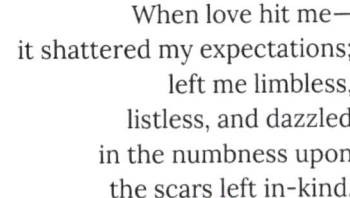

When love hit me—
it shattered my expectations;
left me limbless,
listless, and dazzled
in the numbness upon
the scars left in-kind.

So, I ponder in the
tympanic notes of your voice—
the tones that
beckoned my soul.

You are my Novalunosis,
my over-consuming supernova,
and yet, I sit still in
the paean and bask in the sunshine
you have left behind.

Reticent, I cannot find
sadness in your joy,
as our sweet memories
engendered harmony undefined—
even as I lay in the remnants of your loss.

Angela Psalm

SUPERCILIOUS SOLICITUDE

My heart lays in your soul like:

Arctic snow upon heart chords.

*As a beloved's diary written upon
a glacial noose that held a severed heart.*

*A mist of crimson apathy
of weaving webs of vampiric gloom.*

Yet, even time cannot take
the magic of the moment.

We have danced within a new dawn
in vestiges of sepia—or black and white.

You, my love, are my king of swings,
even amongst the spring that sprung sorrows.
It is instilled in grey windows of truth beyond
hers, his, or our eyes.

In our memories, we were the children of tomorrow,
and the adults of today.

DACITE, DARKNESS, AND DIVINITIES DIALOGUE

We've become a knot in the heartstrings,
chained by sundrops on carnations,
twirling like a typhoon, we are
an emotional, weathered temperament.

I am in love with your light
and you are the light of my dark ways.
I have watched the passion of your soul filtered
through my kaleidoscopic eyes.

We are engulfed in the songs of a Siren—
unable to avoid the enchanting hands of death.
We do not lie in wilted fields,
or on the canvas of dove-white threads,
or in the words of my sadness,
or in your down-casted pen.

continued...

Angela Psalm

If stars were gold, you are the lambent universe—
our tenebrous cosmic sky,
not an intricate infatuation,
but an effulgent blazing fire.

You are the periwinkle of faith,
and I, a persimmon of luck and longevity.

Yet, that was then,
           this is now,
and after all the time that has passed
           within our immortality.

Here we are.

The only constant was the everlasting adoration.

We've walked through the labyrinth
of your twisted mentality.
We are not sophisticated sojourners,
we are a home rewriting
with palm leaves of victory and eternal life.

DACITE, DARKNESS, AND DIVINITIES DIALOGUE

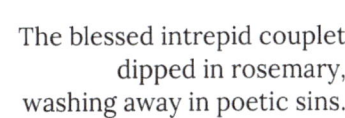

The blessed intrepid couplet
dipped in rosemary,
washing away in poetic sins.

Endlessly sewing shadows
while healing the pain
that we have endured.

Like every avifauna has its nest,
we have returned—
not unlike a robin's visit.

Hope through the arms
of the merciless moonflowers—
our spirits soar.

Or will we be dolphins
in a timeless reef;
and I a lost girl living a life of fear?

Assure me we will not be
ships floating on The Dead Sea
staring into each other's souls.

Hold me close
so that every inch of our skin
is tethered to our touch.

RESCUE ME.

Angela Psalm

SHE IS THE NIGHT

I have been asked, *What is love?*
My answer is, *Death.*
All laid in the emptiness of your viridescent eyes,
as they stand still in the aged polaroid reflections—
a curled edge buried in unfathomable lies.

Everything else was lost within the black-laced heart
and let loose in the sorrowful winds—
where animated kites soared high in the sky,
buoyed by a disintegrating, fragile vessel.

There, my wounds pretended they were healing—
sutures dissolved into seeping wounds of the unfeeling.

Watching each word wage war
and fall apart in the tormented rain.
The essence of petrichor no longer brought peace,
nor salvation, only pain.

We could have had it all, but it was never meant to be—
not in this lifetime at least.

Reality was too abrasive on my skin,
I loved living in my head 'cause
it's a prettier mess than the world.
I sought comfort in my antechamber of inner peace,
in his whispered breathless echoes.

She is the derecho,
She is the temenos,
She is the night's hidden manifesto.

DACITE, DARKNESS, AND DIVINITIES DIALOGUE

TRANSPICUOUS TRANSGRESSIONS

Dear Sunlight,
Be liberal with my skin.
Fill me with the happiness that I cannot grasp.
Funny how distance is no match for memory,
but I have felt the cool touch from
a Gemini dissection of two halves.

Over the years I have learned
that a paper represents more,
Its physical form grants permanence
to my emotional servitude.

My menagerie of inner demons beating
against their caged war
as the day bleeds innocence
into crimson drones—because of you.

I am a mess of black flame
and rose-gold bones of rigidity.
A list of unpublished thoughts
which unfurl into a blossom of pain.
A prisoner of unwanted advances,
only asking to be set free.
A fissure of a forsaken soul,
where her tarragon has been slain.

Now answer me,
*How does it feel to take the light
of the only one you could love?*

Angela Psalm

DIVINE RUINATION

Dear Paramour,

I suffocate in 3 am thoughts,
buried in the pain of solitude.

I shudder to love a forbidden dream
or all matters of muse—
I have gripped Love's throat
and muffled its lies under my restless fortitude,
I have watched the farce of the unrequited,
and have become the victim of it, too.

My heart is a crematorium of scattered ashes,
while I snuffed eternal affection.
I have made love inside the undeserving mouths
of acrid orators purging lies.

Love was never really meant for people like us;
who bathed in nefarious blood.

Eros rested his lavender wings
upon the pillow of her unrested soul,
and she cried.

Like a cultus devotee,
you fed me spoonfuls of elixir dust
to enhance Cupid's illusion.

Where a beating apparatus should be—
there's a void inside of me that can only
be curbed by your presence, not your absence.

I know how to love in pieces,
as this is the form I find myself
each time I step into your shadow of delusion.

DACITE, DARKNESS, AND DIVINITIES DIALOGUE

We made promises under the midnight sky,
blinded by the shooting stars.
Perhaps that is why they never came true,
as they crashed and burned under the sacrificial moon.

I have anguished and watched you tear me
into the scuffle of abhorrent qualms.
I have buried the caskets of your illicit affairs
only to find all those parts of you I rue.

I have locked the door to the hues of magic
that hide the facade of sorrow,
only to find a trap door
with your venom-filled words.
I remember what it was like to bask in heaven's glow,
now it is the path that leads me to death row.

As I sit by myself talking to the moon in my lunacy,
can you picture my predicament?
Watch it unfurl on the bed of nails;
called broken promises—
with bittersweet cosmic screams.

Goddess, soak me in moonshine spirits;
set fire upon my reaped, and violated starlit world.

Angela Psalm

POMELO DEJECTION

*Fill me up with pirouetting dandelions
so I don't drown in the agony.*

I am the void within a pericardium derision,
a damaged and deviated indecision—
slicing straight down the torso of dying dreams.

Fill in the spaces of your insightful measure.
Advance on me in your exceptional visceral cuisine.
As you set fire to my soul, Lucifer takes over in possession;
cooled only by your exotic ocean aquamarine.

Open yourself up to all misadventures,
ubiquitous to my personal conjectures.

Rhyme or reminisce, either will do inside this lost angel,
obsessed in your obsidian, storm-filled control.

You are the flavour of love, my licorice-aniseed rush,
let me languish in your dark pool of lush.
Olfactory or devoured taste, I can never get enough of you.
Validate me post-haste, you are my absolute truth.

I have learned that time does not care for our hearts;
when love fosters lesions and creates chasms.
Where the integumentary lining is enveloped in venom—
a hallucinogenic emotional miasm.

Endear me, my one sweet love—take away this broken heart.

DACITE, DARKNESS, AND DIVINITIES DIALOGUE

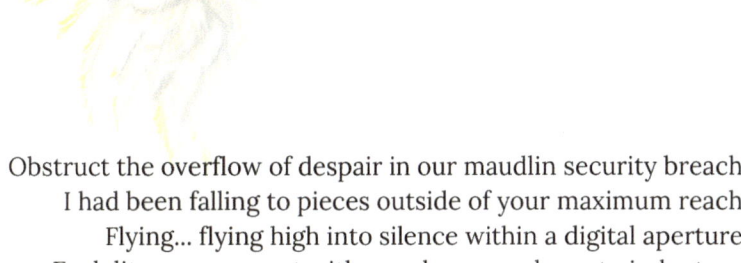

Obstruct the overflow of despair in our maudlin security breach.
I had been falling to pieces outside of your maximum reach.
Flying... flying high into silence within a digital aperture.
Each literary moment with you drew me closer to indenture.

Here, the woe whispered in the wind, and I suffocated.

I cannot take it.

You were the first who broke my heart of trust,
We were steeped in misery, where our thirst could never be sated.

I cannot shake it.

Our cobbled path has led us down to a field of flowers—
now plucked, which lay bleeding, and avulsed.

GLOSSARY

WORD	DEFINITION
A	
Abhor	Regard with disgust and hatred.
Ambling	Walk or move at a slow, relaxed pace.
Anaesthesia	Insensitivity to pain, especially as artificially induced by the administration of gases or the injection of drugs before surgical operation.
Anatomical	Relating to bodily structure.
Apathy	Lack of feeling or emotion: impassiveness, lack of interest or concern: indifference.
Artifice	Clever or cunning devices or expedients, especially as used to trick or deceive others.
Aspiration	A strong desire to achieve something high or great.
Avalon	Celtic Mythology, the isle of the dead, an island paradise in the west where King Arthur and other heroes are taken after death.
B	
Befallen	Especially of something bad, happen to someone.
Belligerent	Hostile and aggressive.
Benignity	Kindness or tolerance toward others.
Betrothed	The person to whom one is engaged.

WORD	DEFINITION
C	
Cadence	Has come to mean "the rhythm of sounds" from its root cadere which means "to fall." Originally designating falling tones especially at the end of lines of music or poetry, cadence broadened to mean the rhythms of the tones and sometimes even the rhythm of sounds in general.
Carnations	Carnation meaning varies depending on the flower color. But at its heart, basic carnation flower meaning embraces the ideas of fascination, distinction, and love.
Carotid	Relating to or denoting the two main arteries which carry blood to the head and neck, and their two main branches.
Catacombs	Insensitivity to pain, especially as artificially induced by the administration of gases or the injection of drugs before surgical operation.
Caterwauling	Relating to bodily structure.
Cathartic	Lack of feeling or emotion: impassiveness, lack of interest or concern: indifference.
Celestial	Clever or cunning devices or expedients, especially as used to trick or deceive others.
Cephalic	A strong desire to achieve something high or great.

WORD	DEFINITION
C	
Chrysalis	Celtic Mythology, the isle of the dead, an island paradise in the west where King Arthur and other heroes are taken after death.
Cierge	A wax candle, especially one used in religious ceremonies.
Circumnavigating	Sail or travel all the way around (something, especially the world), go around or avoid an obstacle, avoid dealing with something difficult or unpleasant.
Clandestine	Kept secret or done secretively, especially because illicit.
Coagulate	A fluid, especially blood change to a solid or semi-solid state. Cause a fluid to change to a solid or semi-solid state.
Coalescence	The joining or merging of elements to form one mass or whole.
Coitus	Sexual intercourse.
Conjectures	An opinion or conclusion formed based on incomplete information.
Consigned	Deliver something to a person's keeping. Send goods by a public carrier. Put someone or something in a place in to be rid of it or them
Constellational	Of or having to do with a constellation.

WORD	DEFINITION
D	
Dejected	Low in spirits: depressed.
Dejour	Of the day.
Delirium	A mental state in which you are confused, disoriented, and not able to think or remember clearly.
Despondent	Feeling or showing extreme discouragement, dejection, or depression.
Detritus	Waste or debris of any kind. Gravel, sand, silt, or other material produced by erosion. Organic matter produced by the decomposition of organisms.
Diabolo	A Greek word often translated as Devil.
Dirge	A lament for the dead, especially one forming part of a funeral rite.
Disbandment	The act of no longer operating as a group; the act of making somebody/something no longer operate as a group.
Discourse	Written or spoken communication or debate.
Divertissement	A dance sequence or short ballet usually used as an interlude, an instrumental chamber work in several movements usually light in character, diversion, entertainment.
Dolour	A state of great sorrow or distress.

Word	Definition
D	
Dysphoria	A state of feeling very unhappy, uneasy, or dissatisfied.
Dryad	In Greek mythology, a nymph or nature spirit who lives in trees and takes the form of a beautiful young woman. Dryads were originally the spirits of oak trees (drys: "oak"), but the name was later applied to all tree nymphs. It was believed that they lived only as long as the trees they inhabited.
E	
Efficacy	The power to produce a desired result.
Effulgence	The ability to shine brightly.
Elliptical	The omission from speech or writing of a word or words that are superfluous or able to be understood.
Elysium	A place or condition of ideal happiness.
Embodiment	A tangible or visible form of an idea, quality, or feeling.
Embouchure	The way in which a player applies their mouth to the mouthpiece of a brass or wind instrument, especially as it affects the production of the sound.
Engendered	Beget, procreate, to cause to exist or to develop produce. policies that have engendered controversy.
Ephemeral	Lasting for a very short time.

Word	Definition
E	
Epicentre	The central point of something, typically a difficult or unpleasant situation.
Epistles	A poem or other literary work in the form of a letter or series of letters.
Eros	The Greek god of erotic love.
Eschews	Deliberately avoid using; abstain from.
Euphoria	The experience (or affect) of pleasure or excitement and intense feelings of well-being and happiness.
Evanescence	Comes from the Latin evanescere meaning "disappear, vanish." has a quality of disappearing or vanishing.
Eviscerated	To take out the entrails of, disembowel, to deprive of vital content or force, to remove an organ from (a patient) or the contents of (an organ).
F	
Fervent	Having or displaying a passionate intensity.
Fetid	Smelling extremely unpleasant.

WORD	DEFINITION
F	
Fettered	Restricted / confined.
Fidus	Trusty, trustworthy, dependable, credible, loyal, faithful, steadfast.
Flagitious	Of a person or their actions criminal; villainous.
Flailed	Wave or swing wildly, beat, or flog.
Fluorescent	Vividly, colourful.
Foreordination	Being determined in advance; especially the doctrine.
Forlorn	Pitifully sad and abandoned or lonely.
Frankincense	A fragrant gum resin from trees of a genus (Boswellia of the family Burseraceae) of Somalia and southern coastal Arabia that is an important incense resin and has been used in religious rites, perfumery, and embalming.
Fraudulent	Obtained, done by, or involving deception, especially criminal deception.
Freya	A noble woman." It is the name of the Norse goddess of love, beauty, and fertility.
Fujisan	An extinct volcano in south central Honshu that is the highest peak in Japan.

WORD	DEFINITION
F	
Funebrarum	Death, Darkness, Horror, Brutality.
Fusillade	A series of shots fired, or missiles thrown all at the same time or in quick succession.
G	
Gaia	Is the personification of the Earth. Gaia is the ancestral mother—sometimes parthenogenic—of all life.
Gloaming	The time of day when it is becoming dark but is not yet fully dark.
Gossamer	A fine, filmy substance consisting of cobwebs spun by small spiders, seen especially in autumn.
H	
Hades	The Greek god of the underworld. the underground abode of the dead.
Harbingers	A forerunner of something, a person or thing that announces or signals the approach of another.
Hieroglyphs	A stylized picture of an object representing a word, syllable, or sound, as found in ancient Egyptian and certain other writing systems.
Hypnos	In Greek mythology it's the personification of sleep.

WORD	DEFINITION
I	
Icarus	Classical Mythology. a youth who attempted to escape from Crete with wings of wax and feathers but flew so high that his wings melted from the heat of the sun, and he plunged to his death in the sea.
Illuminate	Make (something) visible or bright by shining light on it; light up, help to clarify or explain.
Impetus	The force or energy with which a body moves.
Incessant	Of something regarded as unpleasant continuing without pause or interruption.
Inclination	A person's natural tendency or urge to act or feel in a particular way; a disposition.
Ineffectual	Not producing any significant or desired effect.
Iniquity	Immoral or grossly unfair behaviour.
Injurious	Causing or likely to cause damage or harm.
Insidious	Proceeding in a gradual, subtle way, but with very harmful effects.
Intrepid	Fearless; adventurous (often used for rhetorical or humorous effect).

WORD	DEFINITION
I	
Inveracity	A lie.
Iridescent	Showing luminous colours that seem to change when seen from different angles.
K	
Kintsugi	Also known as kintsukuroi (golden repair), is the Japanese art of repairing broken pottery by mending the areas of breakage with urushi lacquer dusted or mixed with powdered gold, silver, or platinum; the method is like the maki-e technique.
Kismet	Fate; destiny
Kronos	Greek mythology a Titan, son of Uranus (sky) and Gaea (earth), who ruled the world until his son Zeus dethroned him. Roman counterpart: Saturn.
Kyphotic	A curving of the spine that causes a bowing or rounding of the back.
L	
Labium Superius Oris	The upper and lower lips.
Labyrinth	A complicated irregular network of passages or paths in which it is difficult to find one's way; a maze.
Languishing	To be or become feeble, weak, or enervated.
Lethargy	A lack of energy and enthusiasm.

WORD	DEFINITION
L	
Leviathan	A sea monster, identified in different passages with the whale and the crocodile.
Lexicon	The vocabulary of a person, language, or branch of knowledge.
Limbic	A system of nerves and other structures in the brain that controls many of our emotions.
Linguistic	The study of human speech including the units, nature, structure, and modification of language.
Lothario	A man who behaves selfishly and irresponsibly in his sexual relationships with women.
Luciferian	Lucifer worshiper.
Luminescent	Emitting light that is not caused by incandescence and that occurs at a temperature below that of incandescent bodies.
M	
Macarism	An ascription of blessedness; a blessing.
Maelstrom	A powerful whirlpool in the sea or a river.
Maenad	Female follower of the Greek god of wine, Dionysus. The word maenad comes from the Greek maenades, meaning "mad" or "demented." During the orgiastic rites of Dionysus, maenads roamed the mountains and forests performing frenzied, ecstatic dances and were believed to be possessed by the god.

WORD	DEFINITION
M	
Malcontent	A person who is dissatisfied and rebellious.
Manifests	Show (a quality or feeling) by one's acts or appearance; demonstrate.
Manifold	Many and various. a pipe or chamber branching into several openings.
Maudlin	Self-pityingly or tearfully sentimental.
Melancholia	Severe depression characterized especially by profound sadness and despair.
Mellifluous	(Of a sound) pleasingly smooth and musical to hear.
Menagerie	A collection of wild animals kept in captivity for exhibition.
Miasm	a noxious influence or the infectious principle, or virus, which when taken into the organism may set up a specific disease.
Miniscule	Extremely small; tiny.
Monochromatic	Palette composed of one color.
Monograph	A treatise on a particular subject, as a biographical study or study of the works of one artist. a highly detailed and thoroughly documented study or paper written about a limited area of a subject or field of inquiry: scholarly monographs on medieval pigments.

WORD	DEFINITION
M	
Myopic	Medical not able to clearly see objects that are far away: affected with myopia.
Mysticism	Belief that union with or absorption into the Deity or the absolute, or the spiritual apprehension of knowledge inaccessible to the intellect, may be attained through contemplation and self-surrender. Vague or ill-defined religious or spiritual belief, especially as associated with a belief in the occult.
Mythos	The complex of beliefs, values, attitudes, etc, characteristic of a specific group or society. another word for myth, mythology.
N	
Nebulous	In the form of a cloud or haze; hazy. Or (of a concept) vague or ill-defined.
Noumenon	(in Kantian philosophy) a thing as it is in itself, as distinct from a thing as it is knowable by the senses through phenomenal attributes.
O	
Obeisance	Deferential respect, a gesture expressing deferential respect, such as a bow or curtsy.
Oblivion	The state of being unaware or unconscious of what is happening around one, amnesty or pardon.

Word	Definition
O	
Oeuvre	The body of work of a painter, composer, or author, a work of art, music, or literature.
Opalescent	Colourless or white like an opal or changing colour like an opal.
Opus	A separate composition or set of compositions. an artistic work, especially one on a large scale.
Ordinance	An authoritative decree or direction.
Oscillate	Move or swing back and forth in a regular rhythm, vary in magnitude or position in a regular manner about a central point.
P	
Paradigm	A typical example or pattern of something; a pattern or model. A set of linguistic items that form mutually exclusive choices in particular syntactic roles.
Paraesthesia	The sensation of tingling, burning, pricking, or prickling, skin-crawling, itching, "pins and needles" or numbness on or just underneath your skin.
Parenthesis	A word or phrase inserted as an explanation or afterthought into a passage which is grammatically complete without it, in writing usually marked off by brackets, dashes, or commas, an interlude or interval.
Perfidy	The state of being deceitful and untrustworthy.

WORD	DEFINITION
P	
Pericardium	A fluid-filled sac that surrounds your heart and the roots of the major blood vessels that extend from your heart.
Peroration	The concluding part of a speech, typically intended to inspire enthusiasm in the audience.
Petrichor	A pleasant smell that frequently accompanies the first rain after a long period of warm, dry weather.
Pheromones	A chemical substance (as a scent) that is produced by an animal and serves as a signal to other individuals of the same species to engage in some kind of behaviour (as mating).
Prologue	A separate introductory section of a literary, dramatic, or musical work, an event or act that leads to another.
Propitious	Giving or indicating a good chance of success.
Proteus	Greek myth a prophetic sea god capable of changing his shape at will.
Psamathe	Sand-Goddess from the Greek words psammos (sand) and theia (goddess).
Psithurism	Blowing through trees and rustling their leaves.
Psychosis	A collection of symptoms that affect the mind, where there has been some loss of contact with reality.

WORD	DEFINITION
P	
Psychosomatic	Relating to, concerned with, or involving both mind and body.
Pteroglossal	Bird - pteron meaning "feather" with glōssa meaning "tongue".
Pulchritude	Beauty
R	
Refulgent	Shining very brightly.
Reincarnated	Having been reborn in another body
Repertoires	The whole body of items that are regularly performed, a stock of skills or types of behaviour that a person habitually uses.
Reticulated	Constructed, arranged, or marked like a net or network, (of porcelain) having a pattern of interlacing lines forming a net or web.
Reverence	Deep respect for someone or something, regard or treat with deep respect.
River of Styx	Is a river in Greek mythology that formed the boundary between Earth and the Underworld (often called Hades which is also the name of this domain's ruler).
Ruination	Destruction achieved by causing something to be wrecked or ruined.

Word	Definition
S	
Sanguine	Optimistic or positive, especially in an apparently bad or difficult situation, blood red.
Sarang	Korean word for love or affection.
Scabbard	A sheath for the blade of a sword or dagger, typically made of leather or metal.
Semblance	The outward appearance or apparent form of something, especially when the reality is different.
Sentient	Able to perceive or feel things.
Sepulchre	A small room or monument, cut in rock or built of stone, in which a dead person is laid or buried., lay or bury in.
Shekhinah	The presence of God in the world.
Sidereal	Of or with respect to the distant stars.
Solaris	Of the sun.
Solstice	Either the shortest day of the year (winter solstice) or the longest day of the year (summer solstice) either of the two points on the ecliptic at which the sun is overhead at the tropic of Cancer or Capricorn at the summer and winter solstices.
Stratosphere	Lies above the earth's weather and mostly changes very little. It contains the ozone layer, which shields us from the sun's ultraviolet radiation except where it's been harmed by manmade chemicals.

Word	Definition
S	
Stygian	Very dark.
Subjugate	Bring under domination or control, especially by conquest, make someone or something subordinate to.
Subluxation	A partial dislocation, slight misalignment of the vertebrae, regarded in chiropractic theory as the cause of many health problems.
Surveil	To carefully watch a place or person or listen to private conversations over a period of time, usually in order to get information about illegal activity.
Synapses	The site of transmission of electric nerve impulses between two nerve cells (neurons) or between a neuron and a gland or muscle cell (effector).
Synaptic	Able to perceive or feel things.
T	
Taciturnity	The presence of God in the world.
Tartarus	Of or with respect to the distant stars.
Temperance	Moderation in action, thought, or feeling, restraint, a habitual moderation in the indulgence of the appetites or passions.
Tenements	A type of building shared by multiple dwellings, typically with flats or apartments on each floor and with shared entrance stairway access.

WORD	DEFINITION
T	
Thanatos	In Greek mythology, Thanatos is a figure who represents death. In psychoanalysis, Thanatos is a person's urge toward death or self-harm.
Threnody	A song of lamentation for the dead: elegy.
Transcendent	Beyond or above the range of normal or physical human experience, higher than or not included in any of Aristotle's ten categories.
Transgressions	An act that goes against a law, rule, or code of conduct; an offence.
Translucent	Permitting the passage of light.
Traversing	Travel across or through, move back and forth or sideways.
Tumultuous	Making an uproar or loud, confused noise. excited, confused, or disorderly.
U	
Ubiquitous	Present, appearing, or found everywhere.
Unconsecrated	Not having been made or declared sacred: not consecrated, buried in unconsecrated ground. an unconsecrated offering.
Unscrupulous	Having or showing no moral principles; not honest or fair.
Untethered	To confined or restricted with a tether.

Word	Definition
U	
Ursa Minor	Lesser Bear constellation located in the far northern sky.
V	
Vacuous	Having or showing a lack of thought or intelligence; mindless, empty.
Vampyr	Alternative form of vampire, undead creature.
Vermillion	A vivid reddish orange, a bright red pigment consisting of mercuric sulphide. broadly: any of various red pigments.
Vesper	Evening prayer.
Vestal	Virginal / innocence.
Vestige	A trace or remnant of something that is disappearing or no longer exists.
Vexatious	Causing or tending to cause annoyance, frustration, or worry.
Vigil	Present, appearing, or found everywhere.
Viridescent	Not having been made or declared sacred: not consecrated, buried in unconsecrated ground. an unconsecrated offering.
Visceral	Having or showing no moral principles; not honest or fair.

Word	Definition
V	
Vomitus	To confined or restricted with a tether.
X	
Xenial	Hospitable, especially to visiting strangers or foreigners.
Z	
Zephyr	A soft gentle breeze.

Angela Psalm

ABOUT THE AUTHOR

Angela Psalm (@angela_psalm) is a Melbourne, Australia, based poetess who started writing at the tender age of 10 years old in her journals to make sense of her emotions and social landscape.

While traversing through her love of sci-fi, fantasy and adventure books, particularly books on Arthurian Legend her favourite was Marion Zimmer Bradley's retelling 'Mists of Avalon', Jane Austen collections. She found her love of sonnets in Shakespeare and the incredible Bronte Sisters, in her mournful sadness.

While still very much in love with writing, she gave up after she was told that she would never succeed by a Mentor at the age of 20. Crushed, she stopped writing. During that period away from writing she continued to consume books, losing herself in their stories and journeys while she went into a career in Holistic energy work and remedial massage as well as business.

But during the covid lockdown she found herself back into journal writing trying to find herself but instead of losing herself in the darkness she used it as a tool to find herself again in writing.

On Instagram in August 2020, a platform of belonging / sympatico, she found lifelong friends and all-encompassing love of poetry, reading other poets words.

While her writing style can be dark and / or sensual,
it's only in search of light.

To connect find her on Instagram: @angela_psalm

ABOUT THE ILLUSTRATOR

SueAnn Summers is an illustrator, poet, and writer from upstate New York. Having discovered the magic of transformation through art and writing at a young age, her spark for creating bloomed into a full-blown passion. SueAnn began selling her paintings in a gallery at the age of eighteen. Since then, she has studied various mediums, techniques, and styles to create unique works of art for her diverse clientele. While serving in the USN Seabees, she painted a large mural of the Seabees Memorial, which still hangs today in Pearl Harbor, Hawaii. From small details painted on egg ornaments, stationery, and book cover art—to full illustrations and wall art—it is clear to see the love she puts into each piece of her beautiful work. With each creation she sends to its forever home, a piece of her heart will be attached.

To connect with SueAnn, find her on:
Instagram @the_musing_palette.

ABOUT THE CO-EDITORS

Kindra M. Austin

Kindra M. Austin is an author and freelance editor from Michigan, USA. She is a mother to a human star and proudly married to an ARMY veteran. When she has weekend afternoons to herself, she likes to visit hill-top cemeteries and photograph headstones, turn-of-the-century and older. She always leaves a token at the gate upon arrival and exits in reverse so no spirit can follow her home.

Austin's published works are comprised of two novels and six books of poetry. She is presently working on a fantastical thriller series when she's not studying for her CPhT certification. Her writing often employs the darkness of loss and grief, and she marries those emotions with acerbic wit. She has found a home in the indie sea of publishing, and she is dedicated to helping her fellow gothic creatives sail.

She dislikes social media, but you can follow Kindra M. Austin on Instagram. Look for @gothic_poser. All her books are available on Amazon and Barnes & Noble online.

Kristy Johnson

Kristy "Kiki" Johnson has an MFA in Creative Writing from the New School, in NYC which infuses her work as a freelance copy editor and writing coach. She has worked part- and full-time as an academic and creative developmental copy editor for going on 22 years.

Her poetry is published and forthcoming in thread litmag, BarBar, New Note Poetry Magazine, The Winged Moon Magazine, Mars Hill Review, Image Journal, in a thousand flowers poetry anthology, among others. Poems based on her trauma recovery journey are featured in Phoenixes: an anthology written by survivors.

For your own editing needs, reach her directly at: kristysjohnsonediting50@gmail.com

Brandy Leigh Lane

Brandy Lane is an poet and publisher in the United States of America and has her Associate of Arts degree from Ball State University. She started her imprint "Where Beautiful Inks" in 2020. She has published five personal books of poetry, two anthologies featuring over 50 writers from all over the planet, and is working with poets, artists, and writers worldwide to help bring words to readers everywhere books are sold. You can find her on Instagram @wherebeautifullives.

ABOUT
WHERE BEAUTIFUL INKS LLC

Where Beautiful Inks is a publishing imprint based in the United States of America. Services include consulting, publishing advisor, formatting, editing, cover design, publishing, mini web design, poetry writing, illustrations (digital collage and hand-drawn), and photography with minor editing.

If you would like more information, please feel free to contact her at the links below (her social media is on the site).

https: wherebeautifullives.my.canva.site poetryandpublishing

https: wherebeautifulinks.com

OTHER PUBLICATIONS WHERE YOU CAN FIND MY POEMS

 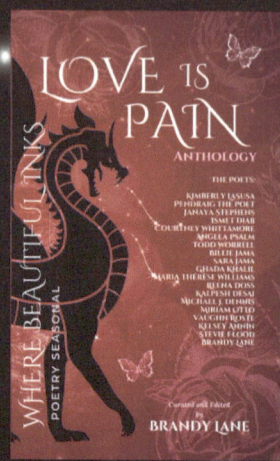

Brandy Lane,
Instagram: @wherebeautifullives

Valerie Lorraine,
Instagram: @valerielorraineproductions